The Lighter Side of Veterinary Medicine

by

Dean W. Scott, DVM

Dedicated, as always, to my wife, Sue, and daughters, Heather and Caitlin, who have been my support throughout the years

Introduction

I have been cartooning longer than I've been a veterinarian. The first ever cartoons I put on paper were upon leaving a job as an assistant technician. On a whim, I got the idea to jot down, with pencil, a dozen illustrations of things that had happened over the year that I had worked there. This was meant as a gift for the veterinarian, Dr. David Webb, who has since passed from ALS in 2008. The first four cartoons in this book are redrawn versions of those original ones. I left Dr. Webb's place in East San Jose, California, for a job in the research area for UC Davis, whereupon I applied for the second time and was accepted the following year into vet school. Many cartoons erupted from those four years and are collected in the two-volume set *Vet School Survival Guide: From the Back Row* and *Vet Med Spread*. Plug: found at Amazon and Barnes & Noble.

I've always believed that we don't have enough humor in this field. While I understand much of what we deal with is serious, I find I can't help my brain that seems to find amusement in most everything. My job is to give you permission to laugh at the things that we deal with on a constant basis in this job. Our burdens and worries are lifted from us for that moment when we chuckle or laugh at something, even if it is ourselves. I hope this book provides that outlet for you. Enjoy!

P.S. I hope to have a sequel to this book out soon, so keep an eye out for it.

These first four cartoons are redrawn from the first dozen that I ever drew. I had not ever put pencil or pen to paper for illustrating before this and could not explain why I thought this was something I could do. I just did it. I rarely draw known people into my cartoons, but three of these are Dr. Webb, moustache and all. I don't know why I changed the name and face on the glove cartoon, because I distinctly remember having done that one with Dr. Webb's visage as well. He was always lamenting not understanding why dogs objected to his anal gland expression procedure and I thought the reason was pretty obvious as seen in the cartoon. The dachshund cartoon is a bit of an exaggeration, but I still have the scar from that particular dog encounter (I don't know why I'm called Bill in this cartoon; not like I change names to 'protect the innocent'). The cat cartoon was based on a little hellion that pulled a Tasmanian Devil maneuver on Dr. Webb, tearing up his arms and back in particular. Did I mention I was still a novice technician? The x-ray cartoon I did because we had to drive 20 minutes to another clinic to take radiographs, not having a machine of our own. We were a staff comprised of three people and Dr. Webb in a tiny strip-mall clinic. Though we were told which views he wanted, invariably there'd be something not quite right or a little off and we'd have to drive again to get more views. This was in the days of dip tanks for processing films too, always a laborious process. And now I just feel like one of those old guys, "Back in our day, we had to chisel our records on to stones! We were happy when they came out with papyrus! Now all you young'uns are going paperless. Consarn technology!" When I gifted the original cartoons to Dr. Webb, I remember he really enjoyed them, more than I had thought he would. That would be the impetus for me to continue cartooning and why this collection exists for you today.

It's going to be ok, little buddy.

Dr. Jones never quite understood why dogs feared him when their anal glands needed expressing.

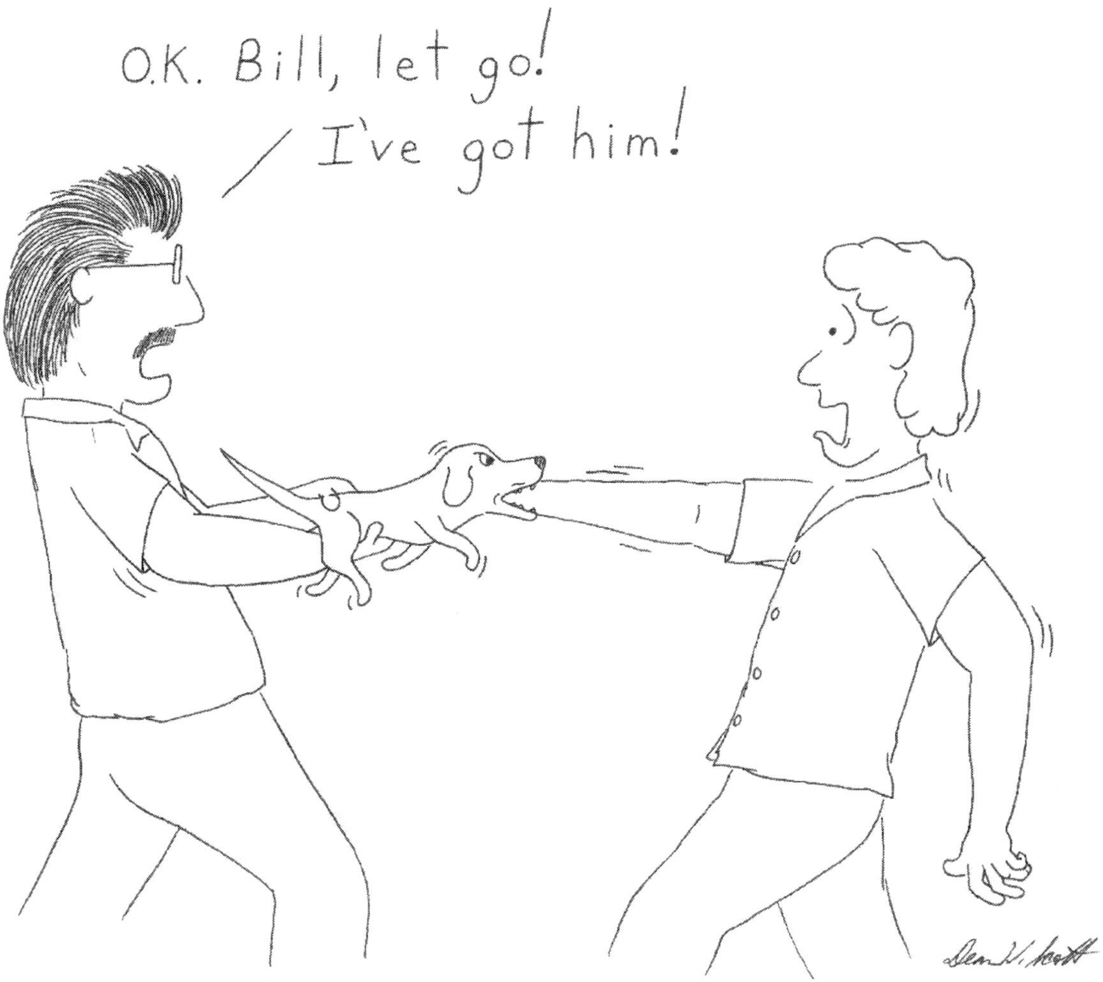
O.K. Bill, let go!
I've got him!

You'll find a lot of familiarity in the following scenarios I'm sure. You'll notice a disparity in the look of many of the cartoons. That's because my "process" is to write an idea down, eventually get to drawing it, then add it to the ongoing stack of cartoons. I've been doing this for over three decades now, so some of these were done many years ago and some were done right up to the time of publication. Some cartoons I did redraw, but many I left in their original form for three reasons. One, I find it interesting to see how my technique has changed (improved?) over the intervening years. Two, I thought they still worked without being redone (I like some of my earlier work because it was a simpler style; just enough to convey the idea). And three, I'm basically lazy. I don't intentionally draw anyone in particular or reference their names. Apologies to all of the Dr. Smiths and Dr. Jones (especially Indiana) out there, as I use those as generic names a lot. The only time I reference someone specifically is when I use my own name. Either it was a particular situation I was involved in or I'm making fun of myself. At the end of the book, you'll find a bibliography of sorts. I thought some of you might be interested in the origins of these cartoons, as for instance the Dr. Webb cartoons. I don't have notes or stories about each one, just where I thought it added value or context to the cartoon. You can certainly appreciate the cartoons without referencing or if you want to check those cartoons out first, hey, knock yourself out. It's your book after all! I hope you enjoy!

Vetless In
Seattle

A Few Good Vets

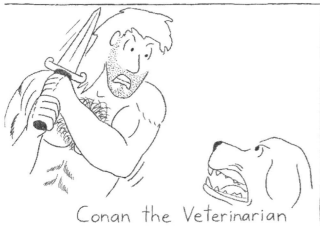

Conan the Veterinarian

Dr. Forrest Gump

13

14

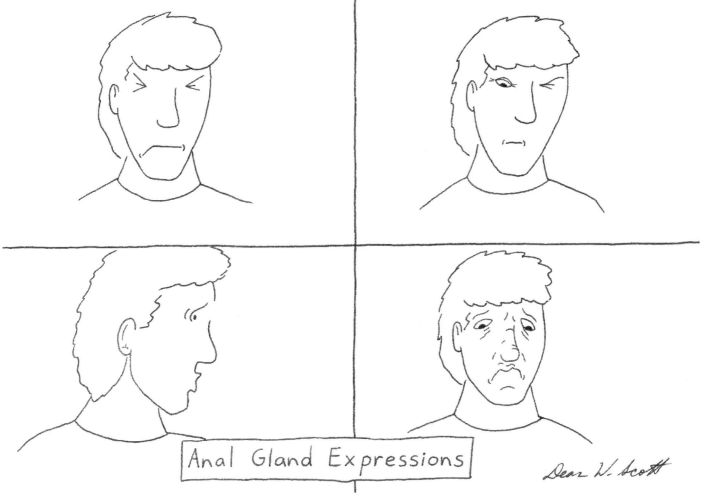

The radiographs show he has a hairline fracture of his radius.

Thanks, Doc! I'm sure glad we had him X-rated!

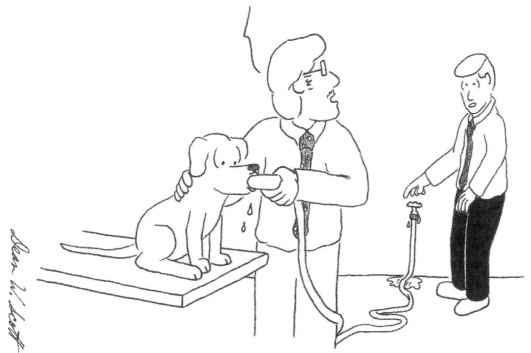

Fluid therapy: the old-fashioned way

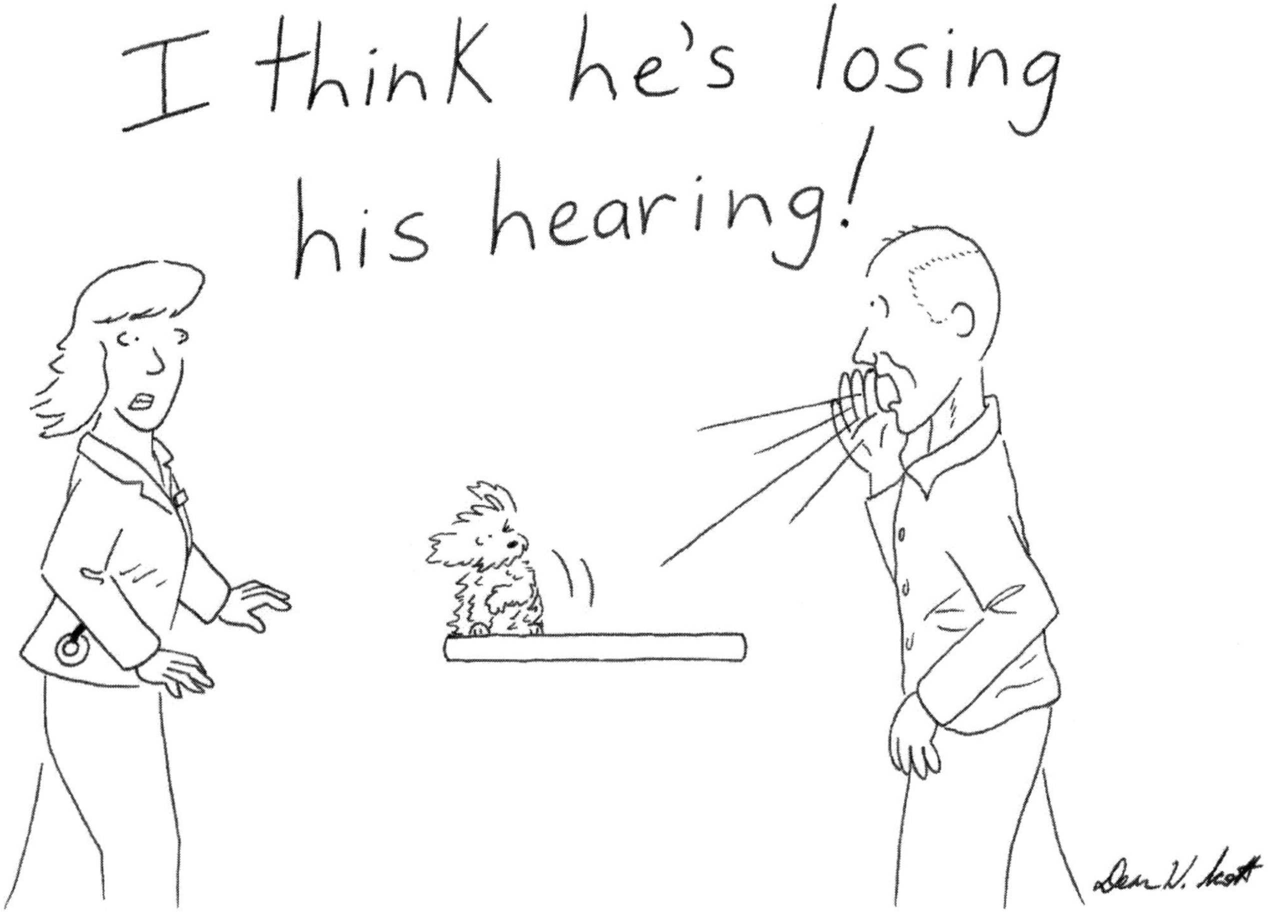
I think he's losing his hearing!

My mother always warned me about guys like you.

"I have a particular set of skills. Skills
I have acquired over a very long career. Skills
that make me a nightmare for people
like you. If you get your pet to a veterinarian
now, that'll be the end of it. I will not look
for you. I will not pursue you. But, if you
don't, I will look for you, I will find you,
and I will neuter you."

Dr. Liam Neeson
Spay & Neuter PSA

24

"My pillow is lovely, soft, and deep.
But I have promises to keep,
Many patients to see before I sleep,
Many patients to see before I sleep."

Dr. Bob Frost's day begins

The Coneheads

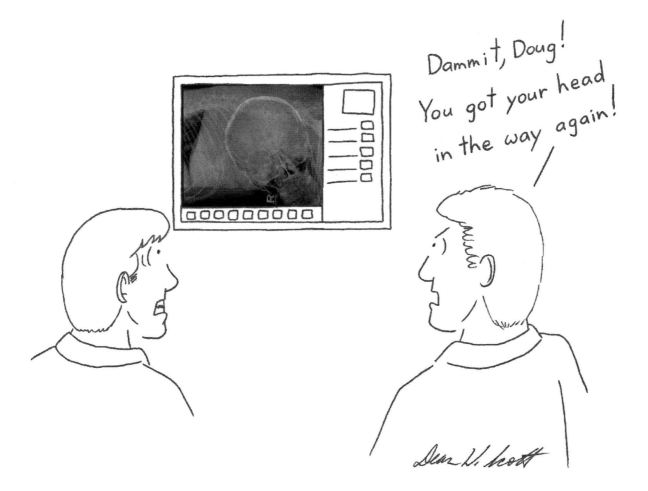

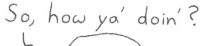

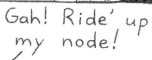

NINJA TONGUE

Good veterinarians
talk to animals.

Great veterinarians
hear them
talk back.

Hey, Barbara, will you come here? I seem
to be having trouble with this new doppler.

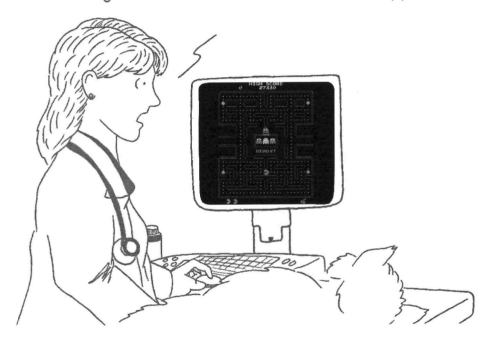

34

He's fifteen in dog years.

Dean W. Scott

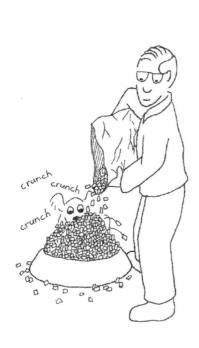

I only feed
him diet food!

Dean W. Scott

36

Today on 'This Old Spay' we have a
sixteen year old German Shepherd cross....

We just got shots at your clinic. I think he's having a reaction! He's blown up like a balloon!

40

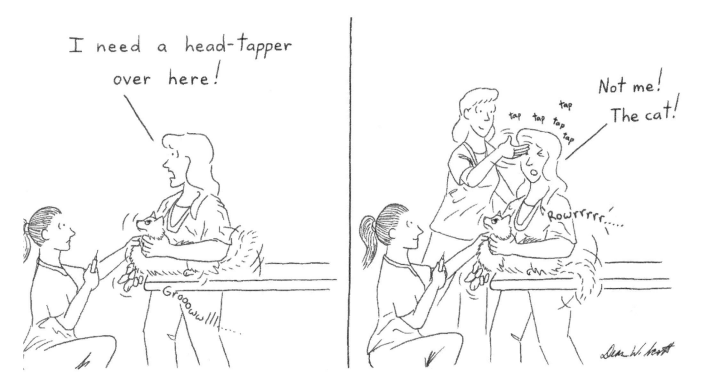

41

He keeps mocking me!

He needs something to calm
him – he doesn't do well in the car.

Screeeechh!!

Dean W. Scott

47

That collar really brings out her eyes!

Dr. Scott's attempt to incorporate complementary medicine into his practice

How to tell when the client-doctor relationship is getting too close.

52

Hey, Dr. Scott! I volunteered here when I was in high school. I stopped by to tell you that my time and experience here talked me out of being a vet! So....thank you! Thank you so much!

Did you have fun at
work playing with all
the puppies and kitties?

Dean W. Scott

Oh, no, I couldn't...
I'm on a diet, remember?

Well, okay, but only
because you insist.

crunch

crunch

crunch

Another? Oh, I really shouldn't.

Dean W. Scott

All right... I guess
another five won't hurt.

Old Vet Vestibular Syndrome (OVVS)

Being bilaterally cryptorchid
Sam suffered from testicle envy

Get a muzzle and rough me up!
Ooooo...that's it, yeah... use a
BIG needle! I've been a bad,
bad, naughty little dog!

Dean W. Scott

73

I think you should clamp that off.
Boy, you're sure taking a long time.
Oh, look there – that's bleeding....

Back-Seat Surgeon

We're not going to know whether
there is or is not a foreign body
in there until we look, Mr. Schrodinger.

Eventually, Dr. Bradley had to put a limit on the number of clinic pets

Dean W. Scott

They're sick!

Dean W. Scott

78

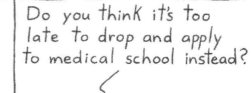

81

Dean W. Scott

88

That last appointment
Kind of reminded me
of prom.

Dr. Smith starts to worry about where he gets his clients

"Dr. Grok, get me a 2 gauge needle."

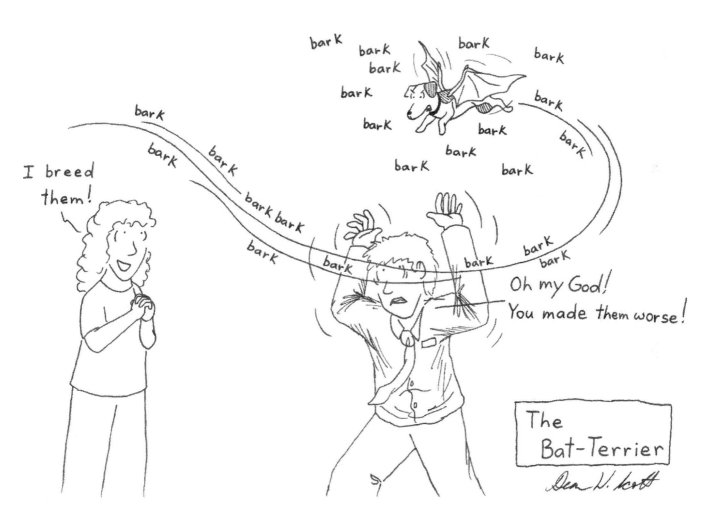

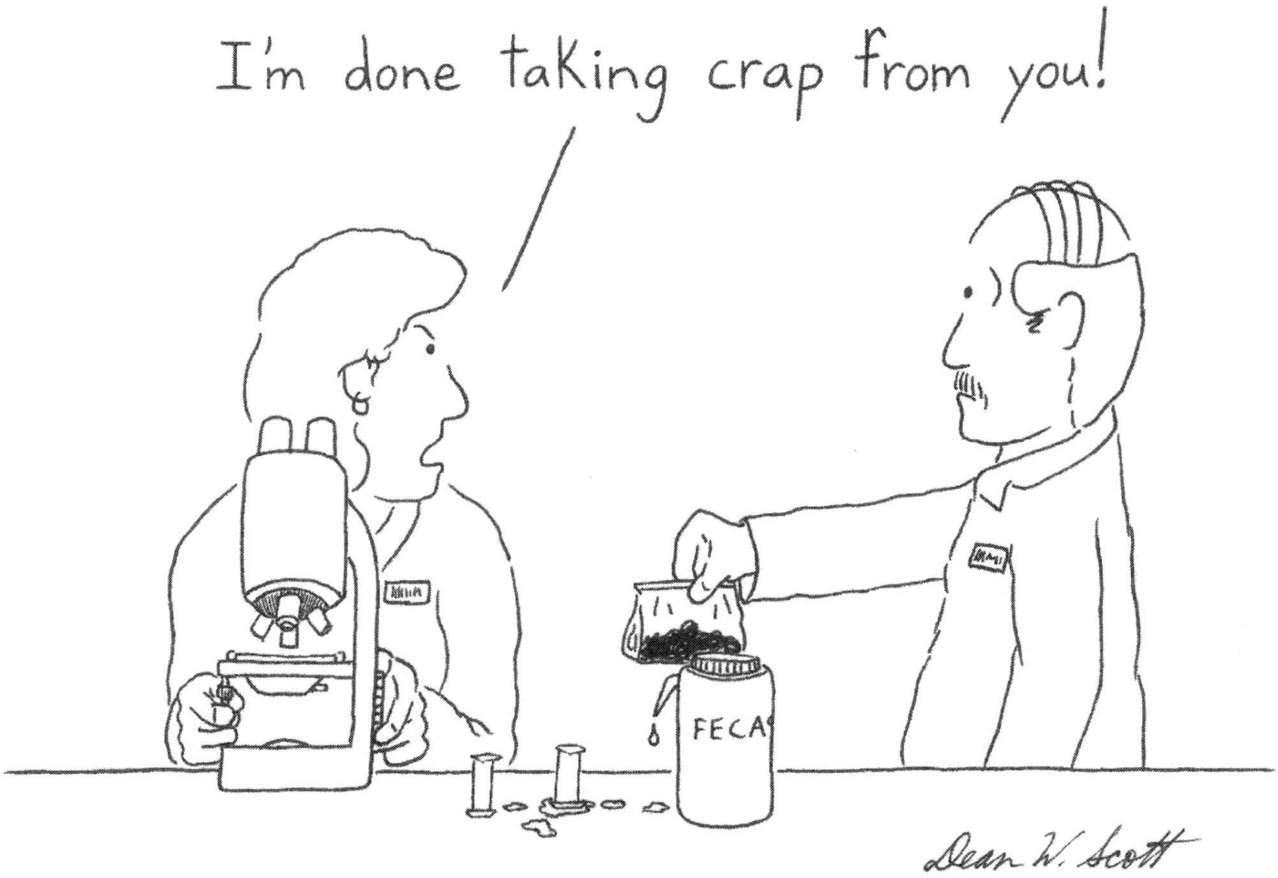
I'm done taking crap from you!
FECA
Dean W. Scott

104

"He's been walking funny."

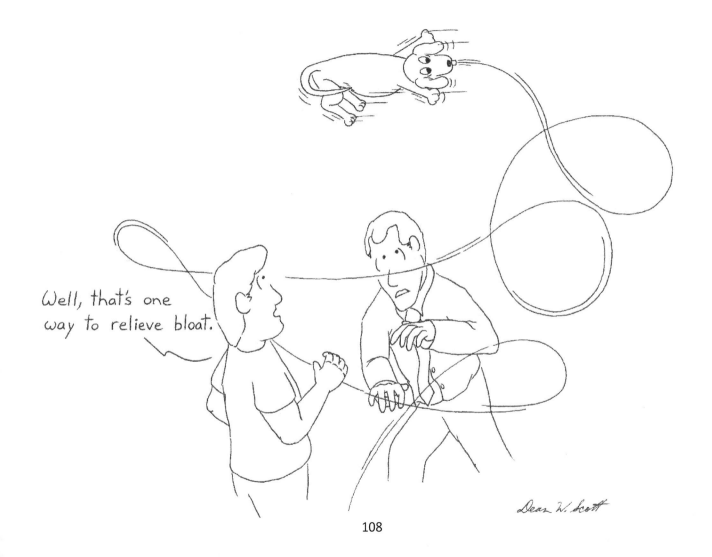

Me? Oh, I'm a veterinarian now. Primarily small animals.

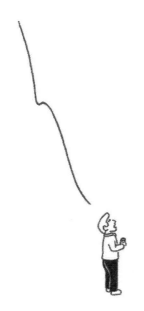

Veterinary genetics

Barney: Before and After Neutering

"Well, though we don't know what zoonotic disease you caught from that dog yet, it's still good you were wearing your mask and gloves."

...... the third step of treatment is BLARRGH

Dr. Jones suffers the embarrassment of lingual cramp

Barney hasn't learned to sit, stay, beg, or shake but somehow has learned to "pants" his owner.

Dean W. Scott

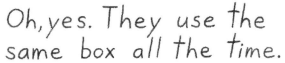

134

135

Her name is Sybil.

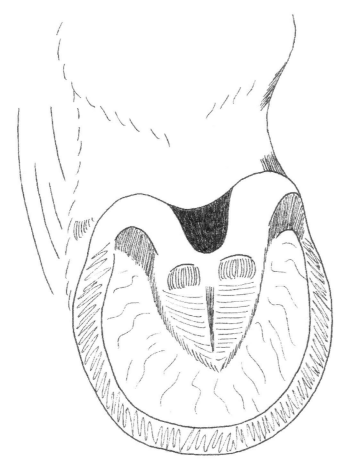

The last thing you see before you change your career.

Dean W. Scott

blah blah blah... liver enzymes... blah blah... possible Cushing's... blah blah test.... blah blah blah... ultrasound....

???

Doctor to Client Communication

"blah blah blah... acronym... acronym... blah blah... multisyllable word said really fast....blah blah... esoteric unrelated fact... blah... acronym... blah blah blah.... unnecessary study reference....

???

Specialist to Doctor Communication

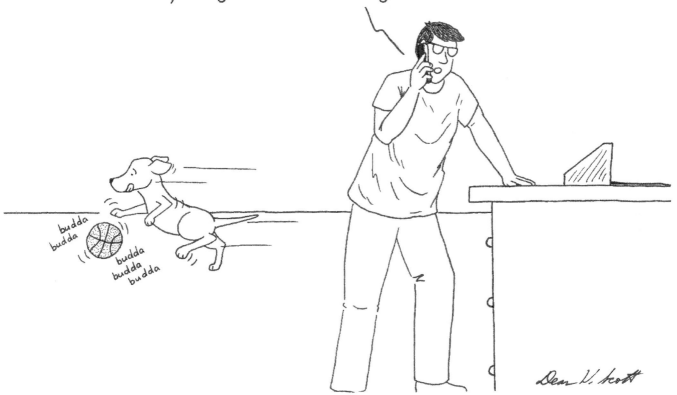

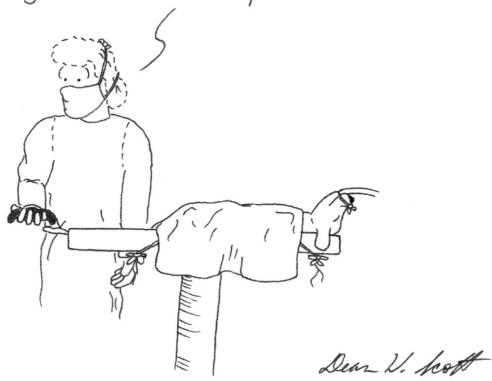

Fist-fighting among veterinarians is unprofessional;
scalpel-fights.... oK.

Dean W. Scott

Guess which one is the future vet
SCOTT
1
VOTOE
9
CHANDLER
8
2
7
Hey, little Kitty!

"You think I need to see a specialist? But your sign distinctly says Large Animal Hospital and I can't deal with his diarrhea any longer!"

Most mice, on average, live about two years. I can only presume his relentlessly cheery nature accounts for his advanced age.

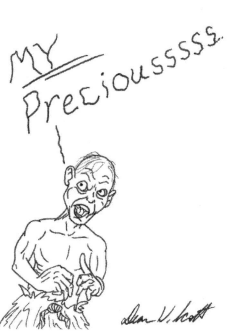

155

Well, yes, I have to admit, this is the first Pitbull-Leg cross I've ever seen.

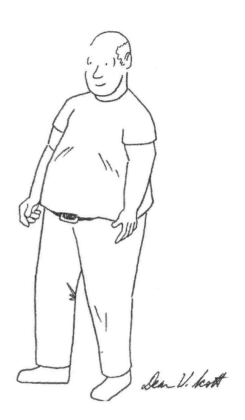

I'm sorry. We can't fix stupid.
We can neuter it. But we can't fix it.

Food Trial

Corn aka Maize, a known and admitted grain, is brought here to answer for its crimes.

158

thump
thump
thump
thump

Dean W. Scott

We have a dog in room one having ingested some marijuana brownies.

Huh. Whadda you know? It's 4:20.

Dean W. Scott

"Sheba" McPherson! You're the next contestant on 'The Vet Is Right'!

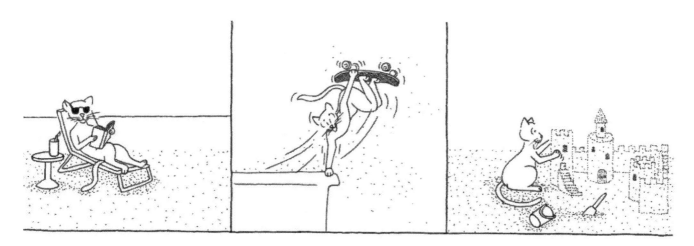

I need to make an appointment. My cat's using the litterbox inappropriately.

Ash finally had to admit the vet was right and Pikachu needed to be put on a diet

174

Did you have your hand in the x-ray beam again?

I'm a responsible breeder! I only breed purebred Labradoodles, maltipoos, morkies, schnoodles, and puggles!

179

Something's wrong. She's being nice.

Which dog had a dental cleaning?

Dean V. Scott

He's been like this ever since you neutered him!

187

Working in an All Cat Clinic can do things to your staff

190

197

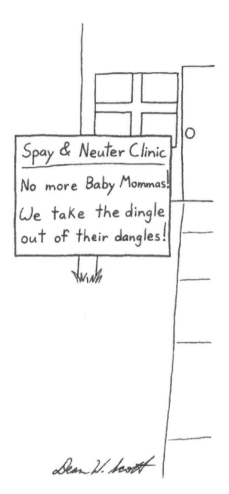

He's lost his groove.

Mobile Vet

Immobile Vet

Dean W. Scott

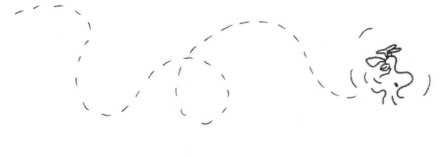

I have a high degree of suspicion that this is Avian Vacuolar Myelinopathy!

Your dog has a congenitally acquired portacaval shunt which did not resolve post-partum. A mid-incision laparotomy to ligate the connection between the caudal vena cava and portal vein can be done.

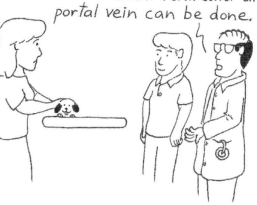

He said, "Your dog's broke. I can fix it."

Veterinary Interpreters

206

208

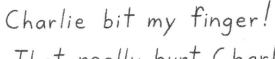

Whipworm

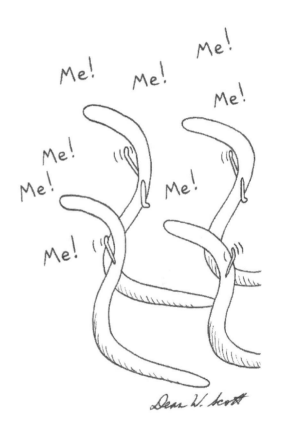

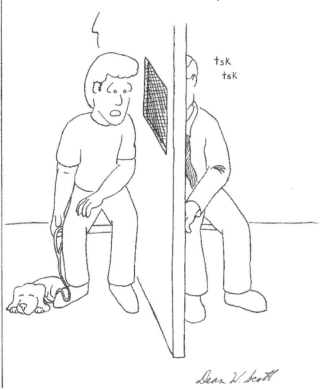

214

Here's volume four of Cricket's chart.

Yes. I really think you
need to neuter.

Dear V. Scott

Yes, it's cute on the internet, but he cantz has cheezburgerz anymore!

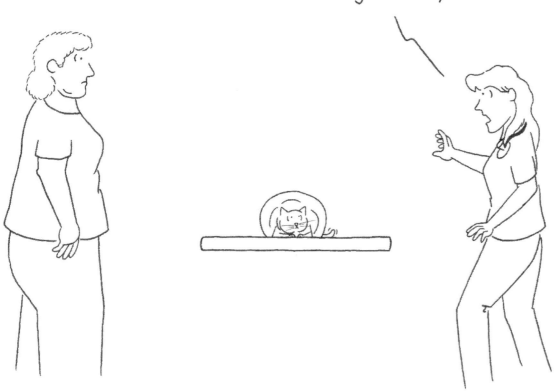

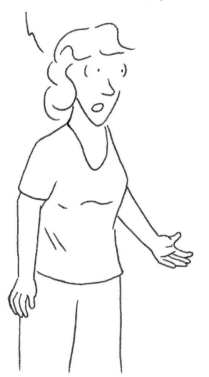

I don't understand. Why did you send me to a veterinarian?

You said you needed a good doctor. You didn't specify what type.

222

Different Containers Feces Come In

MARGARINE TUB

wadded up paper towel

"sealable" bag

DUMP TRUCK

beep
beep
beep
beep
beep

Not-So Happy Meal Bag

He's a small dog. It took us 3 months to get enough.

Dean W. Scott

Max became a bit paranoid after he found out his vaccines were overdue.

Cuterebra

Cutestebra

Dean V. Scott

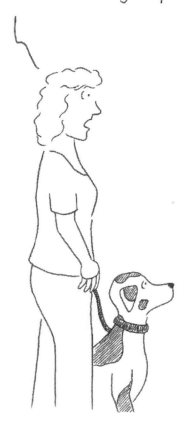

I figured with the big
bucks you make you
could do anything.

M.D.

230

I know what you're thinking, punk. You're thinking "did he trim all four paws or only three?" Now to tell you the truth, I forgot myself in all this excitement. So, you've gotta ask yourself a question: "Do I feel lucky?" Well, do ya, punk?

"Peanut" at 8 years old

"Romeo" at 13

"Harry" at 7 years old

"Zip" at 15

Pets are named when they're young

Before Endoscopes

Dr. Lidofsky misses, of course

"Here. She has us all scheduled to go to the vet's. So, everyone will need to get to their usual hiding places. And don't tell the dog."

Formulating Balanced Fluids

Dean W. Scott

We named him 'Velcro.'

<u>References</u>
(this title makes it sound more intellectual than it is)

Page 13 – I have many movie-related cartoons. I've always been bothered by how little we are represented in films or, when we are, how poorly we are represented. Consider the movie *Outbreak* with Dustin Hoffman. It's a movie about a zoonotic disease. Not a veterinarian to be found! I decided I'd just convert movies to veterinary themes to satisfy myself and this cartoon is the first of those.

Page 17 – I have progressed into being the "old" vet. And it makes me worry if I've gotten complacent or not as attentive as I was when I first started out. This cartoon is what I figure some new, young, still shiny vets think how the grey-haired among them practiced "back in the day".

Page 24 – I woke up one morning with the image of this little guy you see on the table. This happens sometimes where an idea comes completely unbidden to me. I thought he was kind of cute and my brain rarely does cute. But there was no context, just the image. I built the rest of the scene around him with the thought, "Ok, who would take this weird creature to a vet?" And there you have it.

Page 31 – This was one of two cartoons I did as a commission for someone to use in their slides for convention talks. I can't remember what the other one was, but they rejected this one and I thought it was the better of the two. I couldn't do color for this book without it jacking up the price, but I'm sure you can still appreciate the Space Invaders theme.

Page 37/38 – Some cartoons are fun because you can date them to an era from the reference. The "This Old House" reference definitely dates me (no one else will). I wonder when the Captain Marvel reference will become old. It also makes me worry that some people won't get the reference, like when I have to explain to my staff why something I said was funny and give them homework to look up old black and white shows so they'll understand in the future. Because it will come up again.

Page 76 – This is a not completely exaggerated thing that happened. They had named the cat, Jesus, because they had "found" Him. That was the only cute thing about him and his visit.

Page 80 – Except for drawing it, I can't take credit for this one, as a first-year vet school student relayed this conversation to me.

Page 107 – Speaking of references, please don't tell me I have to explain Monty Python to anyone.

Page 124 – This was a cartoon I did while working as a veterinary technician in the research part of UC Davis. There were times we had to take precautions depending on the animals and what studies they were part of. Sometimes it'd be mask, sometimes, gloves, sometimes both, or even more elaborate measures. I thought, "What if the precautions you took only protected those parts of your body, but the rest of you got the problem?" And that's how a cartoon idea comes about.

Page 139 – I wish I did more large animal cartoons, but I have so many just from my little veterinary niche. I think I did this one in vet school and I've found all of the large animal and equine vets think it's funny. If anyone in large animal wants to send me ideas, please do so! I feel like I'm not representing everyone.

Page 154 – I don't know if I conveyed it well enough, but when I thought, "What kind of pet would Gollum have?" the only answer was a hairless cat.

Page 156 – I have no excuse for this cartoon. My apologies for putting this visual in your brain.

Page 176 – Two things about the short film "Feast". One, all I could think while watching it was all of the impressionable children thinking it was perfectly ok to feed their dogs as seen in the film. It came out in 2014, therefore in about 10 – 15 years, these children will be adults with their first new pets and this is the lesson they'll have learned. Two, the damn animated dog was so cute and I fought against liking it because of its message. I hate cognitive dissonance!

Page 187 – Sometimes a lesson sneaks in with a cartoon. This is one. Sorry. I think we need to understand how much goes on in a home that affects a pet's health and we will probably never know. Certainly, in this cartoon, we have all smelled the dog who must be a heavy smoker. However, there are many other things that clients will not share or not think important that could be revealing for diagnosing their problem.

Page 228 – One of the rare cartoons that I did completely on the computer using my drawing tablet. I still prefer to pencil and ink on paper. There's just something more tactile about it. Though digital has its own positives and look.

Page 239 – This was one of those instances where I had the complete idea for a cartoon at once. It was based on how often cat owners have to cancel or reschedule because they can't find or capture their cat. I drew it and then when writing the words, my brain piped up and said, "Hey, add 'And don't tell the dog'." And, that, for me is what makes this cartoon even funnier. I love how my brain offers up ideas even when I'm not actively searching for ones.

Page 244 – I met my wife and daughters at a restaurant directly from work. I had changed my shirt. I'd learned my lesson long ago not to wear scrubs or other medical wear in public. We were seated in a packed part of the restaurant. Before we had even ordered drinks, all of the tables around us emptied out. Coincidence surely! However, I couldn't help but think, "Do I smell like vet?"

Page 246 – I personally think this is a very funny cartoon. It's one of my favorites for the perfect combo of visual and play on words. It also holds a space in my heart because of how someone took offense to it. My family and I were attending an Open House at the University of Florida Veterinary School. We were there shilling for the veterinary student cartoon/humor books and also had cartoon prints for sale. This was one of them. One lady, after perusing the cartoons, felt it necessary to tell me how she didn't think it was funny and she had lost a dog to the same thing shown in the cartoon and that she didn't feel it was appropriate subject matter considering the event we were out. I answered, "Well, I'm sure if you keep looking, you'll find something you find funny." She got a bit huffy and left. She's lucky I'm polite, because what I wanted to tell her was that I did not make the cartoon with her in mind. It wasn't a decision on my part to draw something that would offend, though I find people can find offense in just about anything nowadays. I would have gone on to say, "However, if you truly had a dog with the same problem, then I'd have to say that you are part of the problem, because the not-joke lesson of the cartoon is that people do let things go like that, until nothing can be done. I guess you're owning up to being a bad owner then? This is a confession?" I understand the whims and vagaries of my fellow primates too well. I let it go. Until this book, of course.

If you enjoyed this collection, check out other books by Dean Scott:

The Incomplete Dog Book–Nothing You Ever Wanted To Know About Dogs

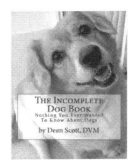

Vet School Survival Guide – From the Back Row

Vet School Survival Guide – Vet Med Spread

Cowabunga – an illustrated children's book

Coming Soon:

Menagerie and Menagerie 2 – animal cartoon collections

The Lighter Side of Veterinary Medicine 2

I also recommend this book "*Staying Sane In the Veterinary Profession*" from our good friend, Dr. Annette Docsway.

It's a half-serious/half-funny book that I'm sure you'll get a lot out of. It, too, has cartoons.

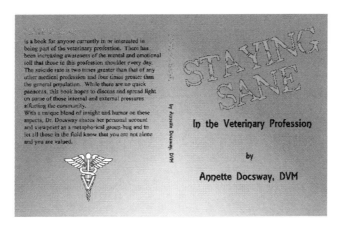

All of these books can be found on Amazon on-line or

at Barnes & Noble, on-line and in-store!

Made in the USA
Middletown, DE
09 October 2023

40512850R00146